PAULA MONTGOMERY

A SUMMER TO GROW ON

Pacific Press Publishing Association
Boise, Idaho
Oshawa, Ontario, Canada

Most names of characters and a few names of places in this story have been changed.

Edited by Marvin Moore
Designed by Dennis Ferree
Cover art by Mark Cable
Typeset in 11/13 Century Schoolbook

Library of Congress Cataloging-in-Publication Data
Montgomery, Paula.
A summer to grow on / Paula Montgomery.
p. cm. — (The Becka Bailey series; bk. 3)
Summary: Becka faces the challenges of being the youngest counselor at a church camp.
ISBN 0-8163-1032-7
1. Church camps—Seventh-day Adventists—Juvenile literature. 2. Camp counselors—Juvenile literature. [1. Church camps. 2. Camps. 3. Christian life.] I. Title. II. Series: Montgomery, Paula. Becka Bailey series; bk. 3.
BV1650.M62 1991
259'.8—dc20 90 22702
CIP
AC

91 92 93 94 95 • 5 4 3 2 1

Contents

To my mother-in-law, Kathy,
for your encouragement,
your example,
your prayers.

Chapter 1

Camp Wautum Woods

By the shores of Lake Mahala climbed a craggy, snow-draped mountain, barely glowing in the starlight. Across the deep, dark water, waves lapped gently at the shore of Camp Wautum Woods. The youth camp lay silent beneath giant pines and firs, their bouncing branches a symphony of soft sounds, playing a lullaby for the slumbering youngsters.

In Girls' Village Cabin 11, Becka Bailey burrowed deep into her sleeping bag. "They won't talk!" she grumbled in her thoughts. "All ten girls—too shy to do anything but stare at one another!"

Becka tried to pray about the situation, but an annoying sound, like a miniature chain saw, kept cutting her sentences into meaningless phrases.

Supper had proved a disaster, her girls all stiffly proper in their blue jeans and sweat shirts. The awkward, quiet table seemed hopelessly adrift in a sea of noisy voices as the lodge swelled with juniors eager for the week ahead.

Becka cringed at how ridiculous she had felt, babbling away, smiling broadly. (Of course, all staff personnel smiled broadly; it was the rule.) She and the girls' director, Maxine—"Max" for short—had tried several ploys to draw the campers out of their shyness, but to no avail.

Cabin worship time was the same. No one talked. No one wanted to pray. All ten girls just stared, their faces looking eerily frozen in the glow of the heater that hung from the ceiling.

Now Maxine slept peacefully across the aisle, while her assistant, Becka, continued to toss and turn.

For years Becka had looked forward to this counselor job—eight years, in fact—back when she had lugged her overstuffed suitcase through the door of Cabin 15's A-frame for the first time. How tiny and scared she had felt then!

"I suppose that's how these poor girls feel," she told herself, and then she remembered how her counselor had put her at ease.

"A great job I'm do . . ." *What is that sound?*

She sat up on the lower bunk and listened more closely. Snoring. *Someone was snoring!*

Becka slipped into her shoes and robe and followed the irritating noise to the top berth of the next bunk. Carrie lay on her back, blowing loud, gurgling sounds from her throat.

Becka eased the girl over onto her side, then settled back on her own bed to take off her shoes.

Sniff! came another sound, this time from across the aisle. Then more sniffling. Now what?

Again, Becka groped through the dark, ending up at Ruzena's bedside.

"What's the matter, honey?"

"I miss m-my mom," the girl stammered, "and I wanna go home."

Becka put her arm around the bulging sleeping bag. "Now, Ruzena, you don't want to go home already."

"Yes, I do!" the pathetic, small voice declared.

Then Becka used her most persuasive whisper. "Think of all the fun you're going to have at camp!"

"I don't want to have fun at camp. I wanna go home."

Becka sighed, then employed the "brainwashing" techniques she had used on her younger brother, Kurt, at times. When those tactics failed, she prayed with the girl and left her with her promise to go to sleep.

Wearily, Becka climbed back into her sleeping bag and reminisced about staff training the week before. She had worked hard alongside other staff members, spreading wood chips, clearing rocks, and cleaning cabins. There were also Indian songs and lines to learn as Hiawatha's sister in a play for campfire. In the midst of their hard labor, however, the young people had enjoyed some special fun every evening.

Becka smiled when she recalled one such event, the spaghetti feed. She had been matched with Geoffrey Blake. His bright blue eyes gleamed impishly as they were ordered to feed each other the entire meal. Becka clumsily dropped spaghetti in Geoff's juice, and they laughed so much their food grew cold. Becka's auburn-haired friend, Beth Gates, sat nearby with Dan Burnett, likewise spooning vegetables into his grinning mouth. Spaghetti sauce and salad dressing smeared most faces before the evening ended.

"Too bad staff members aren't allowed to fall in love with each other!" Becka sighed. "Another rule," she thought in exasperation, "and an unfair one at that." Geoff, a sophomore in college and a music major, would make a fine catch—"such a positive, sweet guy!"

Becka groaned inwardly at the sound piercing the dark. The miniature chain saw was at it again. She jumped up, turned Carrie over, then made swift tracks across the icy floor and back to bed.

"*Brrr!* It sure is cold for late June," she thought. But Texas, where she would attend college, would be warm nearly year-round. Her heart fluttered at the thought of traveling so far from home.

Because Becka had completed her junior and senior grades in one year, she was much younger than most academy graduates. Barely past her seventeenth birthday, she felt quite inexperienced compared to the rest of the Camp Wautum Woods' staff.

"Please, Lord," she began, "help these girls to talk and to learn about one another—and about You. Help Ruzena to get over her homesickness and . . . " Becka fell asleep.

Monday and Tuesday passed quickly as Becka joined in her campers' activities, including photography class, their specialty that week. "Surely, they'll talk now!" Becka thought while hiking a trail with her girls in search of natural objects to photograph. To her dismay, however, the girls dutifully—and silently—followed her and the teacher, clicking their cameras at trees, the mountain, the lake, and anyone who would agree to stand still for them.

"It's as if they're each in some kind of imaginary cubbyhole, hiding from the world," Becka complained to Beth while they curled their hair early Wednesday morning at the shower house. Becka put down her curling iron with a thud. "I feel like a failure already, and this is just my first week as a counselor."

Beth looked sympathetic, but exclaimed, "Count your blessings! I'd gladly trade a few of my live wires. And to be honest, I'm looking forward to five o'clock, when my day off begins."

"That's right! It's my day off too," Becka noted. "Twenty-four hours of nothing but sleep and lying in the sun. No responsibilities!" She finished a last curl and began to brush her dark blond hair. "I'm so tired, Beth. Every night, just as I'm drifting off, Carrie begins her snoring routine."

Her friend grinned mischievously. "And you were just complaining that she never says anything!"

After a good laugh they returned to their respective cabins.

Becka gazed around at her sleeping girls. At least Ruzena was more content—no more homesickness. In fact, she seemed happy in her own quiet way. And all of them did enjoy the lively songs and plays at campfire each evening.

Just then reveille sounded, waking her charges.

"They even stretch and groan shyly," the counselor noted with little amusement.

The day proceeded as before, her juniors obediently taking part in camp activities, but seeming to leave their voices and enthusiasm packed away in suitcases.

Promptly at five o'clock, Nellie Mansfield met Becka at line call. "Go have fun!" she ordered. Nellie, a tall brunette, would substitute for Becka and Maxine the next twenty-four hours.

" 'Bye, girls!" Becka waved to her campers. "See you tomorrow afternoon!"

"At least Nellie would have no problems with her quiet brood," she thought. She smiled at the new confidence she felt. Technically, she was an assistant to Maxine, because as girls' director, Max was often away from her cabin, taking care of camp business. "I think I could handle a cabinful of girls by myself," Becka mused as she packed a small suitcase for her short trek to the girls' staff cabin, where she and Beth would stay.

At ten o'clock that night, after all campers were bedded down, the staff members wandered to the lodge. Upstairs in the loft a special, carpeted place awaited. Here, every Wednesday, they received a spiritual refresher while sharing testimonies and praying for one another and their campers. Pastor Joe, the camp director, usually had some words of encouragement for them during this "praise meeting."

Becka and Beth sat side by side in the candlelight,

adding their voices to the sacred melodies. After those peace-filled moments, Becka felt reluctant to leave, wanting to drink in any leftover blessings.

"Becka!" Geoff's deep voice broke into her thoughts. "It's Don's and my day off too. Would you and Beth like to go to town for some milkshakes?"

Becka's heart skipped a beat. "I don't know." She hesitated. "It's pretty late—and is it legal?"

Beth answered her question. "On our days off we can go and come as we please. All we have to do is tell Dan. So, let's go!" she coaxed. "It'll be our last chance to indulge in junk food for a whole week."

"All right!" Becka agreed.

The four piled into Don Hamada's car and took off for the town about fifty miles away. Moonlight streamed through tall ponderosa pines as they descended the mountains.

Later, when they reached the sleepy outskirts of the city, the foursome found a cafe open and ordered milkshakes.

While waiting for the waitress to return, Becka decided, "I think I'll phone my mother."

"Wish her a merry Christmas for me!" Don called after her.

Geoff couldn't be outdone, so he added, "Tell her, good luck with her scuba-diving lessons!"

Becka giggled. "Hi, Mom! Don says, 'Merry Christmas!' and Geoff says—"

"Becka!" Mrs. Bailey's sleepy voice sounded anxious. "It's after midnight!"

"We're in town, the four of us, Mom. We're recharging our batteries with some junk food."

"Now, Becka, you watch those sweets!" her mother protested.

"Aw, Mom, camp food is so nutritious that one milkshake a week is hardly going to make me come down with typhoid fever or some other rare disease."

"Well, just be sure to brush your teeth when you get back to camp."

Becka stifled a laugh. Here she was, ready to go off to college, and her mother was reminding her to brush her teeth.

"Oh, Becka! It's so good to hear your voice. I've missed you, sweetheart."

"I've missed you too, Mom. How are Kurt and Dad?"

Her mother yawned audibly. "They're fine—working hard, as usual. Kurt's helping Grandma in her orchards."

They chatted a few more minutes, then ended with her mom's pledge to visit the following week.

On the drive back to Camp Wautum Woods, Becka and Geoff talked quietly in the back seat, discovering they shared many common interests—especially a deep love of music. Geoff's honey-colored hair glistened in the dim light as their car made its way up the mountainous road.

Becka remembered the first time she had seen Geoff. She was a senior in academy when his college group of musicians had performed at her school. During his marimba solo his hands turned to a blur over the keys, causing Becka's marimba-playing friend, Marty Webster, to drool with envy.

But that wasn't the only instrument Geoff had mastered. He turned up again at Bible conference, this time his agile fingers stroking the keys of a piano. For two hours he had played any gospel song the teenagers had requested while they encircled him with their voices.

Becka glanced again at the handsome musician beside her as the car neared Lake Mahala. Geoffrey Blake would make a "fine catch" indeed—if only it weren't forbidden by the camp manual.

A few moments later she and Beth said goodnight to

the fellows and made their way to the girls' staff cabin. The next morning both girls slept until noon, then spent a few hours down at the dock sunning themselves. Four-thirty arrived too soon, and Becka slipped into deserted Cabin 11 to unpack. "Nellie's done a good job," she thought as her eyes swept over the neat room. Each bed was meticulously made.

Suddenly, Becka noticed Ruzena's empty bunk. Where was the girl's sleeping bag? She peeked under the bed. Ruzena's suitcases were missing also.

"Oh, no!" Becka groaned, dreading the explanation she knew awaited her.

Chapter 2

The Quiet Ones

Becka hastily dipped into the bag of lollipops she had purchased, placed one on each pillow, then hurried to line call, where Nellie's anxious face met hers.

"I'm sorry, Becka. Ruzena's parents came and took her home today."

"But, how . . . why . . . ?" Becka stammered.

Nellie slipped her arm around the younger counselor's limp shoulders. "Apparently Ruzena wrote them about her homesickness that first night, and as soon as they received the letter they drove all the way up here."

"But she wasn't homesick anymore," Becka protested. "In fact, she was really enjoying camp."

"I know," Nellie said. "After talking with her parents, I feel *they* were the ones missing Ruzena, and when they received her letter they jumped at the chance to take her home."

"Oh!" Becka's spirits plummeted to the sawdust under her sneakers.

Nellie wrapped her arms around her in a comforting, Camp-Wautum-Woods hug. "I'm so sorry, Becka. I did my best to change their minds—and so did Pastor Joe. But it was no use, because they took her home anyway."

"It's not your fault." Becka forced a smile, then turned

her attention to the remaining girls. They looked just as subdued as ever. Would they never perk up and start really experiencing camp life? she wondered.

All through supper an image of short, fairylike Ruzena with her coal-black eyes haunted Becka. She kept mulling over her own performance. "Could I have done something differently that would have encouraged her to stay?" Then she lamented, "I really am a failure my first week on the job. Not only do my girls refuse to interact, but now I lose one!"

Becka's despair followed her like a hovering thundercloud down to the lake that evening for campfire. With junior voices rising in praise songs around her, Becka gazed out over Lake Mahala and beyond the giant mountain, silhouetted against the sunset.

"Are You up there, Lord?" she whispered, breathing a silent prayer. "Things aren't going too well down here. Maybe I *am* too young to be a counselor. But you know how long I've hoped for this chance. I want to become the best counselor Camp Wautum Woods has ever had!"

Geoff had jumped up on stage with his guitar and began leading the campers in a slower tune as Becka prayed, "I really could use Your help, Lord. These girls need to open up and to get the most of their last few days here. Otherwise, I might as well have spent the summer at home."

Just then, Jane, on Becka's right side, snuggled closer. The usual nightly breeze began to puff over the lake and into their faces while they watched the evening's play, and Becka's prayer turned to song, "Praise the Lord, hallelujah." She found herself smiling in spite of her despair. Fellow staff members kept forgetting their lines, and the prompting from the first row became quite obvious with, "Top of page two, Grant!"

"Oh, yeah! That's right!"

Becka noticed a change in her nine girls, also. Not

only were they laughing uproariously at the antics on stage, but several began whispering to one another at times. Her hopes quickened. Perhaps miracles still happened.

After the good-night hymn, her campers waited their turns to pass through the "hug line" before they followed the dark path to Girls' Village.

Becka's juniors seemed more animated that evening as they scurried into their pajamas and robes, then took their places in a circle on the floor for worship. The young counselor turned off the lights, and under the ceiling heater's glow, she began, "Once there was a girl . . ."

When she had finished the story, Becka asked a question, and to her surprise, Carrie (the snorer) piped up, "Well, I think that tells us that we should be careful of one another's feelings. Sometimes just the way we say things can make another person feel bad."

"Yes," Michelle (the plumpish one) chimed in, "we should take time to think like the other person first before we go and say something that might hurt her."

Then Jane timidly added, "Because I was very sick once, I'm really small for my age. And it makes me feel so sad when kids tease me. I can't help my size."

On and on they shared, as if they had kept these secrets locked away for years, only to reveal them that special night. Maxine had tiptoed into the cabin during worship and looked both baffled and pleased at the scene. Later, as an exhausted Becka crawled into her sleeping bag, she whispered, "Thank You, Lord!"

The next morning she snapped off her alarm clock before it woke her campers. Gathering her tote bag, she pulled on her robe and shoes to make her groggy way to the shower house.

"Morning!" Beth called.

"Uh-huh!" Becka responded. She never quite awakened until after her shower.

Back at the mirror and curling irons, the girls discussed Cabin 11's mysterious transformation.

"I'm telling you, Beth, it was as if some angels flew in with that breeze last night and unlocked the minds—and tongues—of every one of my girls!"

"I'm so glad," her friend said. "I just wish He'd *lock* a few of the mouths of my little gremlins."

Becka giggled. "Hang in there! Only two more days to go!"

"And every minute will drag—for me anyway," Beth predicted.

When Becka slipped back into her cabin later, Maxine was just arising.

"Is there any hot water left?" the girls' director asked.

"I doubt it," Becka replied.

"Nothing like an icy shower to wake a person up!" Maxine chortled.

Flopping down on her bunk, Becka noticed a small note floating to the floor. It read:

Dear Becka,

I just wanted you to know that I think you're a really good counselor, and I've enjoyed being in your cabin so much.

Love, Jane

Becka's eyes misted. If nothing else encouraging happened the rest of the summer, last night and this note would make her job more than worthwhile.

Friday marked the final day of photography class, when each girl selected her favorite handful of photos and displayed them in a grand slide show.

The youngsters cheered and "oohed" and "aahed" at various pictures. Becka decided the best shot was of "Pancake," the camp's dog-mascot, kissing Mitch, the water-skiing instructor. Mitch Canwell also played

Hiawatha, Becka's "big brother," in the skit they performed at Tuesday night campfires.

Sabbath School proved different from the usual format. It was a glorified campfire of sorts—in daylight. The program included several skits that illustrated certain biblical principles.

In one act, Dwight Slagle crouched behind cardboard that was painted to look like a power lawn mower. Then the mower began to complain about his owner, how he didn't follow the manufacturer's instructions in what to "feed" him or in other ways that would keep him "fine tuned."

Becka smiled at how craftily Dwight worked health principles into his one-man monologue. She hoped every junior there would take his words to heart, so that none of them would pollute their young bodies with drugs, alcohol, or tobacco, and end up on a "junk pile" like the poor, spluttering lawn mower.

Later some of the actors again forgot their lines and resorted to ad-libbing. Becka overheard Maxine murmur behind her, "Don't worry! It's always this way the first week. Too much to memorize in too short a time! Things will run smoother next week."

In spite of the flaws, the juniors enjoyed the Sabbath School skits. Then they quietly meandered through the woods to the church bowl for the worship service.

Having practiced with the choir several times a week earlier, Becka joined a couple dozen other staff members to sing a medley, chosen especially to create a sacred mood for the occasion. Because the soloist, Kathy Stevens, suffered from a sore throat, Dwight took her place.

The choir's melodious voices rose to the treetops, where even the birds stopped chattering to listen. Then Dwight stepped forward to sing Kathy's part. He glanced at his music occasionally, seeming confident of his role.

But then, without warning, strange words spilled from his mouth—words different from the practiced song.

"What's he doing?" Becka whispered to the girl beside her.

"He forgot to turn the page, so he's making up verses!"

"Oh, no!" Becka gasped, then caught sight of Beth's bewildered face as she gallantly accompanied him at the piano. Dwight sang on, creating his own composition in front of the hundreds of campers!

Finally, the choir resumed its part, and Dwight stepped back into the group, apologizing under his breath with, "Whoops!"

A large laugh deep inside Becka made her entire body quiver, but she didn't dare let it escape. How she wished she could instantly fly a mile away and *har*, *har*, *har*, at the top of her lungs! Then she noticed the twisted faces of others fighting the same urge to laugh. Their angelic expressions remained intact, however, until the end of their performance, when they filed back to their seats among the campers.

Max grinned as if to say again, "Don't worry! Things will run smoother next week."

After dinner the "Walk Through the Bible" was presented. This summer it featured Christ's final week before the Resurrection.

Cliff Schultz had grown a beard especially for the main part and did a splendid job as the mute Jesus before Herod, then in "Pilate's Hall."

Becka acted as one of the guides to escort people to the next Bible episode, ending at last on "Golgotha's Hill" with the crucifixion scene.

The crowd watching hardly breathed as Kendra Locke stepped up to the cross and sang a melody that wrapped around every heart. After she sang of Jesus' resurrection and ascension, the campers were led back to their cabins for prayer and counseling.

That evening only candles lighted the lodge as Maxine quietly explained, "This is an agape supper, a whisper time. It's supposed to be like our first supper in heaven. *Agape* means love—the kind of love God has for us, which we should have for one another."

Becka smiled at "her girls" as they feasted on watermelon, cantaloupe, grapes, plums, and nut breads.

As Sabbath ended with the fading sunlight, the juniors flocked to the campfire bowl for their last evening at Camp Wautum Woods. The play that night brought immediate questions from Becka's brood. "What's going on? . . . What does it mean?"

Because the counselor herself couldn't track any sort of plot, she simply replied, "Just wait. It'll all make sense later." But "later" arrived with one clown atop a milk crate making peace signs, and two hobo clowns receiving food from a kind couple. And somehow a king strolled into the act. Then everyone froze, and that was the end.

"What *was* going on?" Becka wondered, but she never voiced her question aloud for fear of sounding ignorant. She simply told her girls, "It was a profoundly deep play. Really deep!"

The next morning—farewell time—arrived too swiftly for Becka. She helped the campers roll up their sleeping bags and repack their suitcases. Later as she hugged each of the girls before they headed up the bus steps, a dull ache began to swell in her heart.

"Don't forget to write!" she called through the large lump in her throat. Then she turned to Beth and grumbled, "I don't like this part."

"And I don't think it gets any easier to say goodbye, either," her friend warned.

The bus groaned to a start, then pulled out of the parking lot and through the trees.

"Goodbye! Goodbye!" called Jane and Michelle and

Carrie from the windows.

Becka waved one last time, then thought smugly, "Well, if all my campers are that sweet, this is going to be a wonderful summer."

Fortunately, the young counselor had no inkling of the troubles arriving with the next busload that afternoon.

Chapter 3

The Rowdy Ones

The deep carpeting brushed soothingly against Becka's weary legs as she watched the loft fill with other staff members.

Pastor Joe called them to order with prayer. Then a slow grin spread across his face. "Well, let's recap the week. Where were the mistakes? And how can we make Junior 2 camp even better?"

Geoff raised his hand. "I don't mean to sound dumb," he said sheepishly, "but what was the clown skit about?"

The loft erupted in laughter and, "Yeah! What *was* the clown skit about?"

Pastor Joe's wife, Ellen, stepped forward, a blush coloring her tanned face. "We found it hard to convey the deep meaning of that play with just pantomime," she admitted. "Don't worry! We'll work on changing it by next Saturday night."

Later that afternoon Cabin 11's peace was shattered by nearly a dozen babbling girls charging inside and plunking their suitcases down on the wooden floor.

"Oh!" one of them clamored breathlessly. "Isn't Ken Damazo the cutest guy you've ever seen? Did you notice how he grinned at me when I asked him a question?"

Amid swoons and sighs, Becka jumped to her feet, a

"staff smile" neatly pasted across her face. "Hi! I'm Becka Bailey, one of your counselors for this week. Maxine will be along shortly." With a happy lilt to her voice, she continued, "You may choose your beds now, spread out your sleeping bags, and unpack."

All of a sudden everything whirled, and Becka felt trapped in a henhouse filled with a flock of fussing chickens.

"I want the top bunk!"

"No! I want it!"

To make matters worse, there were nine beds for eleven campers. A couple of them would need to use mattresses on the floor.

"*I'm* not sleeping on the floor!"

"Neither am I!"

The prattle continued.

"I won't have problems with nontalkers in *this* group!" Becka thought, then quickly settled disputes and learned the girls' names.

There were Karla and Marelda, the "swooners," who had become instantly infatuated with the camp director's son, Ken. Madge, a short, plumpish blonde, was dragging out her job of bed-making. Sue and Gail seemed to encourage the "swooners." In contrast, Amy and Bernadette quietly put away their belongings. And the remainder, Mary, Larissa, Jan, and Celia, chattered nonstop.

Before line call the counselor gathered her girls into a "huggle"—a huddle of sorts—for prayer.

"But I'm not finished unpacking yet!" Madge whined.

"Hurry!" Becka urged. "We don't want to be late for line call."

They were late for call. They were late for campfire. And the next morning Madge stood helplessly in the center of the cabin wondering how to select her clothes for the day.

"My mom's always told me what to wear and helped me dress," she muttered.

With deliberate cheer Becka said, "Well, you're going to learn some new things this week, aren't you?" When she had finally rounded up everyone for their march to the flag-raising ceremony, she noticed Madge's hair sticking out in every direction.

"Madge, please go brush your hair!"

"But my mom's always done that," the girl insisted.

Some of the campers rolled their eyes in disbelief while the counselor directed Madge back to her bunk and hairbrush.

They were late for flag raising.

"I'm at my wit's end," Becka complained to Beth two mornings later. "Madge is making us late to everything—even to water sports." She sighed heavily. "By the time we get down to the dock, all our choices for tubing and boating are gone. Our cabin has to take leftovers, which isn't much fun."

"Don't fret, Becka!" the other counselor said. "Usually good, old-fashioned peer pressure will straighten a kid out."

"But if the other girls try to hurry Madge, she starts bawling, and that makes us even later. And, Beth—what's Pastor Joe thinking about all this tardiness?"

Her friend made a wry face. "Probably that you're not doing your job. I see what you mean."

"My chances of getting rehired next summer are fading fast." Becka sighed again. "First Ruzena leaves, and now this. Pastor Joe must think I'm dreadfully incompetent." However, Becka didn't find time to worry the rest of that day because her girls bickered constantly. And if they weren't quarreling, they were swooning over some guy.

She felt guilty leaving her brood with the substitute counselor Tuesday evening at line call. Although her day off officially began at five, she decided to stay and participate in the *Hiawatha* play at campfire. After supper she hurried to the costume room to dress in an Indian outfit. She began by smearing reddish brown makeup on her arms, legs, face, and neck. Next she fitted a dark wig with long braids over her blond head. Finally she was ready. On the way she ran into Mitch (Hiawatha) Canwell, and they sneaked together through the trees to the campfire bowl, where the juniors were already singing. They had just walked to the front of the bowl when Becka grabbed Mitch's arm. Mitch turned and looked at Becka with a puzzled expression on his face, but Becka just pointed across the campfire bowl. "Mom!" she gasped.

"What?" Mitch asked.

"That's my mother sitting over there." Becka could hardly contain her glee. "I just paraded past her, and she didn't even recognize me!"

"Well, no wonder!" Mitch retorted. "You don't resemble her fair-haired daughter at all."

After the play Becka stopped briefly by her mother's seat, warning her not to touch her because of the makeup.

"I feel so ashamed," Mrs. Bailey confessed. "I honestly didn't recognize you—my own child!"

Becka grinned. "I'll be back after I try to scrub this stuff off my skin."

The campfire program was just ending when Becka returned to her mother and gave her an official Camp-Wautum-Woods hug.

Mrs. Bailey stayed overnight at Headquarters Building, where she had rented a room. Becka and her mom talked and talked, catching up on over two weeks' worth of news.

The next day they went shopping for college clothes in town. But their time together flew by too fast, and soon the young counselor was waving toward her mom's disappearing car.

Becka shivered in the icy wind blowing down from the mountain. Squaring her shoulders, she hiked bravely to line call to relieve her frazzled-looking substitute.

Madge continued to lollygag, adding fuel to the burning insults already leaping around Cabin 11. To complicate the situation, the weather turned rainy, making it too cold for their water sports classes. Thus Becka and Maxine spent their time refereeing indoor games.

Becka grew so tired from the added stress that she overslept on Friday morning. And instead of the usual reveille, the song "Sleigh Bells" awakened her.

Confused, Becka threw on her robe and peeked outdoors. "Snow!" she gasped. Just then a masculine voice boomed over the loudspeaker, "Happy Fourth of July!"

"It *is* July Fourth," Becka declared. "Wake up, kids! It's snowing!"

All eleven campers crowded past her and into the girls' village, frolicking around in the snow. But as the sun brightened through the haze, the falling snow turned to an unrelenting drizzle.

"Another day of indoor games," Becka murmured. Then she began to help her girls find warm clothes among their summer things, playing peacemaker again for the minor quarrels that erupted.

By suppertime, Cabin 11's boredom and pent-up energy had evolved into giddiness. Karla, Marelda, Sue, and Gail kept jumping up from the table to deliver notes to various fellows throughout the cafeteria. When they managed to drag Ken Damazo back to their table, bedlam broke out.

"Oh!" Karla cooed. "Look at how the salad dressing is dripping down his chin. Isn't that cute?"

Marelda agreed, making annoying clicking sounds with her tongue.

Ken's eyes pleaded with Becka to help him escape this awkward situation. But she simply flashed him a you-asked-for-it look in return.

Suddenly, Marelda and Sue jumped up to find a male slave of their own.

"This is it," Becka said as sternly as she dared. "You will *all* sit down and not leave the table for any reason!"

Karla glowered at her, and some of the others mumbled under their breaths, but Becka held her ground. Pastor Joe had warned of these times when the counselors would have to be firm, yet still radiate a Christian spirit.

"I don't feel very Christian at the moment," she thought.

Sabbath was supposed to be the spiritual climax of the entire week, but Becka felt as if her girls were caught in a sinking, runaway speedboat headed for the deepest part of Lake Mahala. All during the "Walk Through the Bible," Becka prayed for her girls. "It's the last day, Lord. Please influence them . . ."

The beautiful passion of Christ, however, didn't seem to stir the flighty ones, and Becka's spirits hovered at an all-time low that evening at the agape supper.

Maxine had just explained that this was a whisper dinner, when moments later their table grew into a din of voices.

"Girls! You must quiet down," Becka pleaded. "Pretend you're in heaven."

The final blow came when Pastor Joe told Becka she would have to take her girls back to the cabin. "They're just too noisy," he said.

Humiliated, the teenager herded her juniors out of the lodge and up the hillside to the girls' village.

"Help me, Lord!" she prayed. "Don't let me show my anger."

"Everyone into your bunks!" she ordered. "No one is

going anywhere. And we'll remain silent until campfire, which is one hour away."

Moments later, Karla started to wiggle in the bunk above Becka. Then the wiggles quickly turned to giant flip-flops.

"Karla! Please be still!" she said.

The girl's whiny voice singsonged, "But I've got to scratch my mosquito bites."

Becka forced herself to use her calmest, cheeriest voice. "Karla, dear, you'll settle down, or instead of campfire tonight you'll stay in the kitchen and mop floors."

The top bunk froze in place. After about ten minutes Becka got up and asked the girls to join her in a circle on the floor. All did—except Karla and Marelda, who slumped in a corner and pouted.

"OK, girls!" Becka began. "We've obviously not been getting along this week. What do you think the problems are?"

A long silence followed. Then Bernadette's soft, sweet voice came to the rescue. "Some of us have been mean to each other. Instead of saying nice things, we're pointing out faults."

Karla and Marelda shifted uneasily in their corner, pretending not to listen. Several other girls spoke about the boy-crazy attitude and their refusal to obey the counselors. By then sniffling sounded from the corner. Karla and Marelda were sobbing.

Becka's voice filled with compassion. "Would you like to join us?" she asked.

With the suddenness of a summer storm, the dam of pent-up feelings broke. All at once, everyone was talking, confessing, and apologizing amid tears and hugs. A renewed group of girls from Cabin 11 trooped down to campfire that evening—on time!

The next day as Becka watched her juniors leave, she

reflected sadly, "If I had just confronted them the very first night instead of the last, how different our week might have been!" She vowed to apply this lesson to her next group of campers. "Before anything spoils the harmony in our cabin, I'll get them to share their feelings."

"Becka?" Maxine startled her. "Did you know you were assigned to the laundry this week?"

"Laundry?" Becka felt her face flush with bewilderment. "Oh, no!" she thought. "Pastor Joe has lost all confidence in me as a counselor and has exiled me to the wash house."

Chapter 4

The Laundry Room

After staff meeting, Becka gathered her courage and faced Pastor Joe. "Please, tell me truthfully," she said. "Assigning me to laundry—was that a punishment?"

"No!" the camp director replied. "You're doing a fine job. It's just that Sandy Campbell was supposed to be a counselor, but because of a scheduling mistake, she ended up in laundry. Now I'm giving her a chance to fulfill her dream for a week."

New vigor sent Becka hiking to the wash house, where Sandy greeted her with a friendly smile. "I was told to brief you on the peculiar quirks of each machine," she said.

Instructions followed about which washers filled too fast, which needed prodding, and which danced and jiggled their way into trouble.

"The dryers take forever," Sandy explained. "And don't get discouraged! You'll never catch up. Someone's always bringing in more."

Becka's brown eyes grew large at the mounds of clothes stacked everywhere, some wet, some clean and folded, others soiled and waiting for a vacant tub. As soon as Sandy left, she set to work on a couple of sweaters that needed hand-washing. She plugged the deep sink and turned on the faucet, dumping half a cup of detergent into it.

"Hi!" She heard a familiar voice behind her.

Startled, she turned and found Geoffrey Blake's blue eyes beaming into hers.

"Thought you might be lonesome, so I brought you a cheer-up gift." He presented her with two wedges of cold pizza.

Becka giggled. "Thanks! But where did you find these?"

"My day off began last night," he said, "and Don and I found a pizza place."

Becka sunk her teeth deep into the decorated crust. "Mmmmm!"

Without warning a different sound emerged from the whirling and sloshing around them—the sound of a waterfall.

"The sink!" she gasped, racing toward the overflowing tub. Soapy water cascaded down the side and was splashing onto the cement floor.

Geoff quickly found a mop and began guiding the river toward the drain in the center of the room.

"You're getting off to a great start, Becka!" he teased.

The girl blushed as she dipped her arm deep into the sink in search of the plug.

Geoff stayed to mop the floor while Becka did the hand-washing and finished her pizza.

"That's just the appetizer," he told her. "Now it's time for lunch."

"I don't think so," Becka said. "Look at all these clothes!"

"You're coming to lunch, young lady!" Geoff grasped her shoulders and pushed her through the doorway. "You'll need lots of energy for this job."

Soon the two of them sat eating with other staff members, who were discussing "the heater incident."

"What heater?" Becka asked.

"Well," Mitch Canwell began, "ever since staff training, Pamela's cabin heater hasn't worked right."

"Yeah!" Dan Burnett cut in. "She complained and complained to maintenance, telling them how cold the cabin was, but Jack Roland put her off, saying it was all psychological. 'It's not really cold,' he said. 'You just *think* it's cold.' "

Mitch took over with a sarcastic tone to his voice. "Pam told him that when you have to chip ice off your sleeping bag to get up in the morning—that's cold!"

A round of hearty laughter broke out.

"What about the heater?" Becka queried. "Did Jack fix it?"

"Oh, he fixed it all right," Dan replied. "He painted the heating element a fluorescent orange, so she would think it was working OK."

"You're kidding!" Geoff retorted.

"I wish I were," Dan said, "because when Pam flipped the switch, that heater hanging from the ceiling went crazy—shot sparks everywhere, making her campers flee outside. Poor Pam thought her cabin might catch fire, but it didn't."

"And that's not the end of the story," Mitch added. "When Karl, head of maintenance, found out about Jack's prank, he snuck into Pam's cabin and traded her heater for the one in *our* staff cabin. Our heater looks warm with its bright orange element, but it's freezing in there."

Dan gazed across the cafeteria at Jack Roland, who was sitting alone at a table. "Needless to say, Jack isn't very popular with us at the moment."

Mitch agreed, saying, "We keep telling him through chattering teeth that it's all in his head. He just *thinks* he's cold!"

Everyone laughed again.

That afternoon Becka had no problem with cold. She kept quite warm in the wash house, its whirring dryers turning the room into a sauna of sorts. And Geoff added a warmth of his own when he arrived with a stereo and stacks of gospel song tapes.

"You shouldn't be spending your day off this way!" Becka protested.

"Oh, but my conscience would never allow me to enjoy an afternoon on the lake, knowing you were in here slaving away," Geoff said while he busily folded towels and stacked them in a basket.

With the stereo filling the room with music, the afternoon passed pleasantly for Becka.

Glancing at his watch, Geoff exclaimed, "I've got to get up to line call and get back to my campers."

"Thanks so much for the company," Becka said, "and for the pizza—and music."

"My pleasure!" Geoff studied her across a dryer door. "Uh, Becka, I was wondering . . ."

"Yes?"

"The weekend after next is our conference's camp meeting, and, well," Geoff stumbled over his words, "Camp Wautum Woods staff is in charge of the youth program there that weekend."

"That'll be fun," Becka replied. "And I'll get to stay with my folks at their tent."

"I'd like to meet the rest of your family," Geoff told her. "But do you think they'd mind if I stole you on Saturday evening and took you out to dinner after Sabbath?"

"Oh!" Becka looked surprised. "Would it be all right? I mean—with the camp rules about dating and all?"

"Sure!" Geoff exclaimed. "It would be like a day off. And I know of this wonderful restaurant where they serve the best spaghetti in town. The place has a nice, family-type atmosphere too."

"Well, if it's not against the rules, I'd like that."

"Good! Believe me, it's not against the rules." Geoff gathered up his stereo and tapes. "See you later!"

Just as he was leaving, Kendra Locke passed him on her way in. "Has anyone told you you're substituting for me this week?" she asked.

"W-what?" Becka stammered.

Kendra looked glum. "As long as I simply had a sore throat, I could remain a counselor. But when I have a sore throat *plus* a rash, the doctor ordered me to stay away from my campers."

"I'm sorry," Becka said sympathetically. She felt guilty, though, because of the glee bubbling inside her. "I'm going to be a counselor again!"

Becka then instructed the other girl on the peculiar workings of each machine and quickly took flight toward where she had last spied the girls' director. That evening after campfire she hauled her suitcases and sleeping bag over to Kendra's cabin and met her new crop of girls. They were the gymnastics group, young juniors eager to tumble and somersault their way to stardom.

Becka fell in love with them at once. The girls seemed spirited, but sweet—especially tall, blond Jenny, who would be baptized that Sabbath in Lake Mahala.

Interestingly, Geoff's cabin of boys also had gymnastics classes, sharing the instructor that week. In a clownish way Geoff helped Becka's few awkward girls gain confidence. He would tumble over in a haphazard cartwheel to encourage them.

"They think I'm faking this," he whispered to Becka. "Actually, I'm dreadful at gymnastics."

"That's what the teacher's for!" the girl responded. "We're just here to encourage them." She wanted to say, "And you're doing a great job, Geoffrey Blake!"

Watching him, she wondered at the way her heart beat a little faster every time he talked to her. "It seems like we're being thrown together," she thought. "First the spaghetti feed, then our day off, and now my substituting for Kendra has brought our cabins together in gymnastics. Could it be that we're supposed to be spending more time together for some special reason?"

Her mind wandered to the following week. It would be a short one, she mused, devoted to a special group of youngsters, many of them "unchurched," some underprivileged.

Then Friday the entire Camp Wautum Woods staff would travel three hours to the conference campgrounds.

Becka smiled. "And Saturday night I'll go out on my very first car date alone—with Geoffrey."

Chapter 5

Breaking Camp Rules

Driving through the main gate at the conference campgrounds brought an immediate flood of memories surging through Becka. Overladen cars and travel trailers moved like a silent caravan past green tents and white-washed cabins. First the junior pavilion, then the kindergarten and primary tents flitted past her car window, all sweet reminders of her youth. To Becka, camp meeting was Christmas in summer: the bustling, happy-faced crowds; the music; the unrestrained child voices; the stories, skits, and sermons.

Children darted in and out of grassy alleyways, playing tag among the elms that shaded campers from the July sun. When the car halted in front of her tent, the girl climbed out and lugged her suitcase onto a miniature porch.

"Becka!" her mother squealed, hugging her fiercely.

"Hi, Mom!" she said. "Where do I sleep?"

Mrs. Bailey showed her the cot that would be hers for the weekend. Then they sat down and talked a long while. As if on cue, friends from academy dropped by, squeezing into the already-bulging tent.

"I thought this week's campers would be the worst," she confided in Heather, a blond schoolmate. "In fact, I expected tough street kids, maybe even dressed in leather and carrying chains."

There was a hint of laughter in Heather's large, blue eyes as she listened.

"Was I surprised!" Becka exclaimed. "Those girls were some of the sweetest ones I've counseled all summer."

"Maybe that's because they appreciated the atmosphere at Wautum Woods," Heather speculated. "I'm sure it's a far cry from what they're used to."

That evening memories seemed to follow Becka as she hiked with a few girls up to the youth tent, where swarms of other teenagers filled the wooden benches under the "big top." Guitars accompanied their spirited singing, and Becka felt free for a few moments—free from her responsibilities as a counselor. She didn't need to remind any campers to be quiet or to hurry or to put on their sweaters. For now she could just be Becka Bailey, ordinary Adventist teen, hovering somewhere between childhood and adulthood and relishing every carefree minute of it.

The street lamps had come on when Becka filed out with hundreds of other chattering young people. She said goodnight to her girlfriends, then hurried to her tent.

"Daddy!" she exclaimed as he entered, and the next instant she threw her arms around her father's broad shoulders.

He grinned at her. "I brought you some health food, Becka."

The girl looked over at the table, where some plump doughnuts goggled back at her from beneath their cellophane wrapping.

"Oooh! Really healthy, huh?"

"Guaranteed!"

Just then, her brother Kurt broke through the blankets hanging in the doorway.

When Mrs. Bailey arrived with Grandma Shirley, they were all there, crammed into their camp-meeting tent as they had been summer after summer in the past. Wistful thoughts overtook Becka. She wished herself a little girl again, wandering the darkened paths with her brother and hiding among the poison oak, waiting to surprise some unsuspecting young passerby. Such fun!—until the poison oak took effect all over their arms and legs. But even that awful itching shared its rightful place among her camp-meeting memories.

Late arrivers motored, thumped, and banged around the tent until midnight, making it impossible for them to fall asleep—except for Dad.

"A truck driver can sleep anywhere," Mrs. Bailey told them.

Just before Becka drifted off, she whispered, "Mom, are you still awake?"

"Uh-huh."

"Would you mind if I went out with Geoffrey Blake tomorrow night after Sabbath?"

Mrs. Bailey asked, "Who's Geoffrey Blake?"

"A counselor from camp. He's just a friend."

Mom's voice turned serious. "This would be your first time to go out alone in a car with a guy, wouldn't it?"

"Yes," Becka replied, holding her breath.

"Well, you're seventeen now and will be off to college at the end of next month. Geoff must be pretty special if he's a counselor—and your friend."

"He is, Mom."

"Then it's OK with me," her mother said.

A faint smile still lingered on Becka's face long after she had fallen asleep.

The following morning the street in front of the Baileys' tent became a hubbub again as people from all over the campground hurried to their Sabbath School programs.

Becka's red, white and blue Camp Wautum Woods uniform stood out among the pastel dresses surrounding her. Although she felt somewhat casually dressed for Sabbath, she also felt proud to be identified as a camp staff member.

The youth tent's sides flapped gently in a warming breeze as she took her place up front alongside other camp workers and helped them lead the spirited song service.

As soon as the singing ended, Becka was free to sit with her parents, who looked a little out of place among so many teenagers. Still, everyone, young and old alike, enjoyed the religious skits, the special musical numbers, and Pastor Joe's comical-but-serious sermon.

Throughout her day of visiting and more meetings, Becka kept thinking about her upcoming date with Geoff. And that anticipation seemed to slow the time to a crawl. When at last he arrived at her tent that evening, she introduced him to her parents, then walked stiffly beside him toward the upper lot, where he had parked his car.

"Hi, Geoff!" she heard. Then a cluster of friends surrounded them, and they talked awhile. Saying goodbye, the couple trudged toward the parking lot again. But once more they were met by another group of friends. Politely they lingered and made conversation.

Hunger and impatience took turns gnawing at Becka's insides. "I wonder if we'll ever get to the restaurant," she thought, nervously shifting her stance from one foot to the other.

Finally, they said farewell, and Geoff quickly led her to his car. "Hurry, before we meet someone else!" he exclaimed.

"Well, you can't help it if you're so popular," Becka teased.

He grinned as he opened the door for her. "It wasn't

just me they were interested in, young lady."

"Young lady! That's the second time he's called me that. Is that what he thinks of me? Like I'm a kid sister or someone?" Becka started to feel uncomfortable, sitting primly in the front seat, waiting while Geoff started the car and guided it through the dusty parking lot to the gate.

He glanced up at his visor, then asked, "Well, how was your day today?"

"Inspiring and fun," she replied in a crisp voice.

Then he asked, "What do you think about the situation in Africa?"

"Wha-a-t?" Becka looked over at a paper sticking out of the car's visor. She reached up and pulled out a lengthy list entitled, "Conversation-starters for Dates."

"Whoops!" Geoff said. "Uh, I borrowed that from one of Pastor Joe's silly sermons."

Becka scanned the list. Under "How was your day today?" and "What do you think about the situation in Africa?" she read such ridiculous questions as, "How do you clip your toenails so beautifully?" and "Do you think Lebanese children should be allowed to eat candy?"

Laughing, Becka felt her tension melt away. "This is just good ol' Geoff," she told herself. "Who cares if he likes me as a kid sister or not?"

When they arrived at the restaurant, he called out, "Hey! Look over there! That's Morgan Scott from camp with his date, Josie. Looks like they're having car trouble."

"Just tell him it's all in his head," Becka quipped. "All he has to do is paint the engine orange, and it'll run fine."

Geoff laughed, but quickly turned sober. "Poor Jack! He'll never live down painting that heater element." Geoff talked briefly to the other couple, offering a ride if they needed it after dinner.

Becka was finally able to eat some spaghetti and enjoy a more serious conversation with Geoff. They discussed their summer thus far, the lessons they had learned as counselors, their upbringing in different environments. Geoff was basically a "city kid," while Becka was raised on a mountain at the edge of a wilderness. Still, he seemed to love the outdoors as much as she did.

When they left the restaurant, the couple noticed Morgan and Josie still sitting glumly in the parking lot, so the two hopped into the car with Becka and Geoff, and Geoff returned them to where their families were staying for the weekend. By that time it was nearly midnight.

"I'd better get back to the campground," Becka said, "or my mother will be imagining us in a gruesome car wreck. She can be an awful worrywart at times."

Geoff grinned as he drove carefully through the darkened streets. "I think most mothers are," he said. "Comes with their job description." Then his deep voice took on a more serious note. "You know, Becka, I've really appreciated our friendship this summer."

"I have too," she replied. "It's been fun."

Geoff continued, "I've been avoiding girls for various reasons. Actually, you're the only one I've gotten close to in the past couple of years."

"I am?"

"In fact," Geoff said, "if it weren't for the Camp Wautum Woods rule, I'd think I was falling for you."

"Oh?" Becka suddenly felt very shy. She found this turn in the conversation totally unexpected.

Then Geoff's voice grew more determined. "I don't care if it's not the Camp Wautum Woods rule, I *am* falling for you," he said.

Becka stared down at the floormat. Then she whispered, "I think the feeling's mutual."

Geoff parked in front of the Baileys' tent, then reached

over and took Becka's hand in his. "You realize this is against the rules?" he said.

"Yes." Becka mustered the courage to look directly into his face. "If Pastor Joe finds out, he'll send us home."

"Or maybe just not hire us back as counselors next year," Geoff added.

"We'll have to be very careful to keep our relationship as platonic as possible at camp," Becka said.

"I agree." Geoff grinned. "And maybe we'll get lucky and have our days off together, so we can go into town for milkshakes." Then he chuckled. "We're supposed to be actors—at campfires. Now we'll see just how good at acting we are!"

Becka said good night, then slipped into her tent. But worry entered with her. She felt uncomfortable about disobeying a rule—however unfair it seemed. In fact, one of her friends had dubbed her "Miss Goody Two-Shoes" once because of Becka's steadfast adherence to every "jot and tittle" of proper Christian decorum.

She had always abided by the rules—well, almost always. There was a night, much like that warm night at camp meeting, when Becka had briefly strayed from the "narrow path." She lay down on her cot and recalled the incident when she and some other seniors had decided to show a few of the teachers their appreciation by "decorating" their porches and yards.

Well armed with rolls of toilet paper, they had crept through the midnight stillness to Mr. Duvall's house first. She and Marty Webster draped streamers around the doorway and windows while their friends worked on the bushes. Becka would never forget her feeling of horror when she spotted her math teacher watching them through a crack in the curtains.

When the door burst open, she thought her heart would stop beating, but Mr. Duvall surprised them by asking, "Would you all like to come in for some hot chocolate?"

"N-no, thank you, sir!" Marty had sputtered. "We have some—uh—important business to take care of tonight."

Mr. Duvall peered at them in his deadpan way. "Well, then, be sure to take care of it *quietly*," he ordered.

"Oh, we will, sir!" Marty promised while Becka tried to fade into the shadows.

She had never taken part in such a prankish deed before, and she hoped Mr. Duvall hadn't lost respect for her that night.

When they continued their "neighborhood improvement program," next at Elder Finlander's house, she caught herself holding her breath, afraid that the Bible teacher would awaken and discover her mischief also.

"He'd be so disappointed in me," she thought.

Becka had tried to justify her behavior by whispering to Marty that their beautiful job would show the teachers how much they loved them. "And we'd never do this if rain was expected," she rationalized.

"Never!" Marty agreed, tying a fluffy bow around a branch. "Rain makes cleanup impossible," he whispered back, then glanced approvingly up at the cloudless sky.

Still, Becka's guilt grew. And when, at the next home, the history teacher suddenly threw open his front door and growled, "Who are you? What're you doing?" Becka and the others fled down the street at top speed.

But the history teacher, a bicyclist and runner, chased after them with ease. Becka could hear the gravel crunching under his swift slippers as she charged toward the greenery alongside the cafeteria and dropped to the ground behind a bush. She could just imagine the headlines in the local newspaper: STUDENTS ARRESTED FOR TRESPASSING, with her name, Becka Bailey, heading the list of culprits. Such a scandal would heap disgrace upon her family's good name.

"Oh! Please, Lord," she had desperately prayed behind that bush, "don't let him find me." Then she added the pledge, "I'll never do anything like this again."

"But you are!" her conscience scolded her. "You're breaking a camp rule by falling for Geoffrey Blake."

"That's an ignorant rule," Becka argued. "No one can help how they feel about someone." Besides, she knew that she and Geoff could carefully control how they talked to each other at camp. Not one overly fond look should ever appear on their faces.

But, she wondered, would they be able to keep their romance a secret from everyone at Camp Wautum Woods—especially from Pastor Joe?

Chapter 6

Adventure Camp

Bleary-eyed Becka stumbled from her bed on Sunday morning long before the first twitters of waking birds. She jogged to the shower house, then returned quickly to pack for her trip back to Camp Wautum Woods.

"A Porsche? You're riding in Sherry McLain's Porsche?" her mother asked.

"In style!" Becka whispered, careful not to waken her grandmother or Kurt.

Moments later her parents stood arm-in-arm, waving her off as Becka scrunched herself into the shape of a pretzel in the cramped back seat of Sherry's sports car.

Geoff, who sat up front, selected a gospel tape for the stereo. He was already acting quite platonic, she noticed, almost ignoring her altogether.

"Good show!" she thought, wriggling into a half-prone position. As uncomfortable as she felt, Becka knew she must sleep during the three-hour journey in preparation for her next group—the "adventurers."

She had heard rumors about adventure campers. These were the youngest ones, the first-timers, the eight- and-nine-year-olds, who loved to shine their flash-lights on hot summer days and wear shorts and sleeve-less shirts on frigid nights. They would bring the largest cans of mosquito repellent, but return home with the most mosquito bites. Mud puddles looked more attractive to them than the camp's swimming dock. And when it came to hikes, they were known to lag behind and scamper off after the first furry creature or slithering reptile they spotted. The counselor had to be ever vigilant, ever counting, ever awake during adventure camp.

Becka smiled, though, at the positive side of these youngsters. They were the innocent, "unspoiled" ones, wiggly bundles of enthusiasm who crawled right into a counselor's heart and stayed there. And they were the hardest ones to say goodbye to when the time came.

Before long, Becka was hugging a little blond-haired friend, Joni, from her home church. "I'm going to be in your cabin this week," the fourth-grader announced proudly.

"I'm so glad," Becka said. She sincerely meant those words. It was as if Joni had brought a little bit of home to Camp Wautum Woods with her.

One by one the campers straggled into her cabin, toting suitcases almost as large as their small selves. Some of them already had the telltale signs of homesickness tugging at the corners of their mouths.

Becka helped them unpack and roll out their sleeping bags. Then she "powwowed" with them in a circle on the floor, explaining the camp rules and describing the events in store. Asking some leading questions, she encouraged each youngster to tell about herself, her family, her home, and school.

All of them warmed to the counselor and to one another without further prompting. "This is going to be a fun week," Becka speculated.

Next she demonstrated a "huggle," saying a special prayer for her girls before their trek to line call.

That night at campfire she looked with amusement at all the flashlights that were "accidentally" popping on and off, especially in the boys' section.

"The rumors were true," she thought with a giggle.

But the next morning Becka didn't feel at all like giggling. She awoke with a fever and a throbbing headache. And her throat burned as if she had gargled with a cup of her grandfather's jalapeño hot sauce. When she tried to unzip her sleeping bag, her arm moved like a block of concrete. Attempting to roll over, she quickly discovered the rest of her felt the same way.

"Ugh! How will I ever make it?" she asked herself. Then her mind shifted into a higher gear. She could ask for the day off today and spend the time recuperating in the girls' staff cabin. But that would eliminate her regular day off on Friday, when she and Geoff had planned to drive to town together.

"There are less than four weeks of camp left," Becka lamented, "and only four more days off. Then Geoff will leave for his college in Washington State, and I'll head for Texas." She sighed, then decided, "No, I'll suffer through, do my job, and try not to complain."

The next few days dragged by at an unbearably slow pace for Becka, while the adventurers lived up to their name. They eagerly experienced every adventure Camp Wautum Woods had to offer: horseback riding, gymnastics, mountain biking, canoeing, and sailing. With every jolt in a saddle, every pedal of a bike, Becka's head throbbed, and her body ached. And when her squealing campers clung to "the shuttle" (a rocket-shaped inflatable raft) behind the ski boat, she cheered them on through a sandpaper throat.

By Tuesday evening her voice threatened to desert her altogether, bringing worry about her role in the *Hiawatha* play. Her voice held out, however gravelly, until Wednesday morning, when it was reduced to a whisper. Her campers came to her rescue, though, listening intently to her every hushed word and minding her to a tee. They tiptoed around the cabin and offered her tidbits of encouragement.

Becka beamed at her girls with gratitude. "What a delightful time to get sick," she thought. "If this had happened a few weeks ago . . ." She winced at the thought.

Maxine had teased her on Monday morning about her "big date" with Geoffrey Blake on Saturday night. "I heard you two were seen at a certain restaurant until a late hour," she said. "Because you were out gadding about and didn't get enough rest last weekend, now you're paying for it."

But on Wednesday, when Becka was starting to edge out of her illness, poor Max came down with the virus, coughing and sniffling and looking so miserable the younger counselor didn't have the heart to tease her in return.

Becka even played nurse to the girls' director and took over some of her responsibilities, allowing her extra time off from the campers so she could repair more quickly.

At long last Thursday evening, Becka's day off, arrived. The next morning, Geoff drove her down the mountain and into town, where she found a phone. In a few brief minutes she recounted her week of sickness and told her mother all about her "sweet, sweet adventure campers."

"Ya-hoo!" she cheered afterward. "My folks are coming up to camp tomorrow for visitor's day—the whole family, even my Grandma Shirley!"

"Great!" Geoff said.

They lingered over their meal a long while, talking about her family, his family, Becka's sick week, and their campers. Then the conversation turned toward the future.

"You know, Becka, only three more weeks of camp remain," Geoff declared sadly. "Then I have to return to my college, and you'll head south. I'll miss you terribly."

"Well, why don't you simply switch colleges?" Becka suggested, surprised by her own boldness.

Geoff's eyes widened. "Oh, my parents would howl. The expense is bad enough already. Can you imagine what they'd say about plane tickets to and from Texas?" He reached across the table and squeezed her hand. "I've got a better idea. What would you say to your attending my college instead?"

Becka wrinkled up her brow in deep thought. Several of her other friends on the camp staff were encouraging her to enroll at their college in the Northwest also.

"I'm a country girl," she reminded him with a deep sigh. "I'd be just as lost on your large campus as I'd be in a big city, Geoff. One of the reasons I selected my college in the first place was because of its smallness." Becka flashed him a reassuring smile. "Maybe next year I'd be ready for a larger college, but not now."

Geoff shrugged, then asked, "Well, would you at least agree to share my worship time with me every morning down by the lake? I'm studying a really good devotional book."

"Don't you think people would suspect . . . " she began.

Geoff interrupted with, "They'd think we're simply two friends having worship together."

"I'd have to get up about fifteen minutes earlier . . . and if Max'll agree to it—sure!"

"Good!" Geoff exclaimed, then rose to pay their bill, leaving Becka to mull over their conversation. "He keeps forgetting I'm barely seventeen," she mused.

Becka could hardly wait until Sabbath morning, when she would embrace each of her family members and show them "her camp." Sadly, because of her responsibilities, that was about all the time they enjoyed together.

As she caught glimpses of them throughout the day,

her heart felt like a rope in a tug of war. She loved her campers and wanted to make their Sabbath the most special day of the week; but she loved her family also and knew this would be their last time together—the five of them—until Christmas.

That afternoon Becka again acted as a guide for the "Walk Through the Bible." She escorted visitors and campers from one scene to the next. All the actors had sharpened their lines and acting skills by then and seemed quite authentic—especially Cliff Schultz, who played the role of Jesus.

When the cruel-faced "Roman soldiers" repeatedly shouted and jeered at him, then heaved the heavy cross onto his bare shoulders, Becka sensed a strange mood among the onlookers. These youngest of campers seemed to glean more from the scenes than their older predecessors had. They stood as still as the pine trees around them, gazing soberly at the soldiers slashing their whips and prodding "Jesus" up the hill. His every step, crunching the sawdust, seemed to cry out, "I did this for you. I did this for you."

Moments later those same "soldiers" raised the cross, revealing the "blood" trickling down "Jesus' " face and oozing from his hands and feet. Cliff looked so lifelike, hanging there, his sweaty and disheveled hair clinging to his brow. It seemed that no one breathed, except Kendra, whose larklike voice rang out over the crowd in song.

Becka gazed up at the cross, at "Jesus," then over at a few of her fellow staff members. "They're crying! This seems so real. This was real," Becka reminded herself, and then she happened to catch a glimpse of her mother's face, also full of tears. Becka smiled over at her. "He did this for us, Mom."

That evening a gentle spirit reigned at the agape supper as the staff encircled each table and sang that cabin's favorite hymn. The candles flickered, lighting each cherub face. Becka thought that perhaps this was indeed a little sampling of Heaven. And she breathed another thank-you prayer for her cabinful of sweet youngsters that week.

Finding it hard to tell her family goodbye that night after campfire, she watched them disappear through the black forest and thought about growing up. She knew this was part of it. She knew she would visit with her family only in snatches from now on. She wasn't a little girl anymore—someone who could bury her face in her mother's or father's shoulder when troubles came. Her mountain home, with its giant fir trees and wildflowers, would only be hers at holiday times.

Confusing thoughts continued to tug at the girl. This in-between stage reminded her of a bird learning to fly, not quite willing to venture from the safety of its nest, but, oh, how wonderful was the promise of the waiting world!

And how would she "fly" tomorrow when Teen 1 camp brought girls who were close to her own age? Would Becka soar, or would she fall flat on her face?

Chapter 7

Teen Camp

Sunlight spattered the blue expanse of lake surrounding Becka and her friend, Ben Smith. Even in a sitting position, Ben's lanky frame seemed to tower above everything. His gangling, basketball-player legs dangled over the edge of the dock, splashing listlessly in the cool water.

"Sure is tough being a 'sub,' isn't it?" he drawled.

Becka sighed contentedly. "Sure is!" The sun warming her back made her feel lazy, and she let her mind linger in a blissful state, free from all responsibility—at least for the moment.

"You two ready to baby-sit?" asked an amused voice behind them.

Becka glanced up at Jake Shepherd, who continued to talk. "I've come to lifeguard—anything to escape digging that ditch for the new water pump!"

"I don't know if I'm ready for these campers yet," Becka mumbled. "Maybe in a couple of years."

"Wh-a-at?" Ben looked puzzled. "You're not *that* tired, are you?"

"No, just a little scared," she replied. "After all, some of these campers are my age and older."

Ben rattled off a Bible quotation: "Let no man despise thy youth; but be thou an example of the believers, in word, in conversation, in charity, in spirit, in faith, in purity." Then he suggested, "Claim that verse as a promise for yourself the next two weeks!"

Becka beamed up at him appreciatively. "OK, I will. Thanks!"

With the theatrical air of a sportscaster, Jake announced, "And there they come, ladies and gentlemen!" Then he chuckled. "And it looks like a couple of the girls didn't read all the rules in the Camp Wautum Woods pamphlet."

Becka scrambled to a sitting position, then groaned at the sight: two colorful bikinis were winding their way through the trees toward them.

"Uh-oh! They definitely missed the small print about one-piece bathing suits only," she said.

"Well, Timothy!" Ben quipped. "What'll you do about this little predicament?"

"First off," Becka declared, "I don't plan to embarrass them. We'll talk privately later. Anyway, T-shirts make great coverups."

She grinned smugly at her fellow counselor, then called to the newcomers, "Over here, girls!"

That afternoon, after she had discreetly settled the bikini matter, Becka launched upon her whirlwind schedule as a "sub" (substitute counselor). No sooner had she memorized the names of each girl in a cabin than she was whisked off to another A-frame to begin the routine anew.

By Tuesday afternoon she found herself splashing beside an overturned canoe among a hodgepodge of squealing girls. Dog-paddling vigorously in the icy lake, she called out, "Come on, campers! Heave to!"

Amid giggles and grunts, her girls uprighted the canoe and began the chore of climbing back in.

"Whew!" Becka gasped. Then she turned to Jake Shepherd, who had just pulled his muscular form out of the water. "How'd we do this time?" she asked.

"Much better," he said.

"I'm freezing," Sheila Preston exclaimed. "This life jacket doesn't help keep a person warm at all!"

Jake grinned at her. "It's not supposed to." Then he handed her an oar. "Let's go, campers! Rowing will warm you right up."

The other canoes followed their lead across the lake.

Sheila Preston, a former schoolmate of Becka's, began to sing, "Row, row, row your boat, gently down the stream . . ." Other oarsmen joined in, and soon all four canoes were gliding across the water in a musical parade.

"This has been so much fun," Becka said to Jake in a breathless voice.

"Is this the same counselor who was trembling with fear a few days ago?" he asked.

"The same one," she admitted. "Oh, sure, teens need more discipline at times, but they laugh at the same things you do, and—and, well, they're just lots of fun."

Jake's tanned face creased into a wide grin; then he boomed, "Merrily, merrily, merrily, merrily, life is but a dream!"

When the canoes reached shore, Becka hastily glanced at her watch. "Oh, no!" she exclaimed. "We'll be late for line call. Hurry, campers! Up to our cabin!"

"But we're always late for line call," protested one of the girls.

"Not while *I'm* your counselor," Becka said. "Hurry! Let's race up the hill!"

Minutes later Becka was tapping her toe nervously while her girls primped in front of their hand mirrors.

"My hair's a mess," mumbled one teenager.

"My face is so sunburned," complained another. "What will Tony ever think of me?"

"Probably that you're late for line call!" Becka said.

"OK, you're all quite beautiful now. Let's huddle for prayer."

Loud protests resounded throughout the cabin.

Becka's hand flew to her frowning forehead. "How did that verse go?" she tried to remember. "Let no man [girl] despise thy youth; but be thou an example of the believers, in word . . . in spirit . . ."

Like a clucking hen Becka gathered her flock together in a circle of prayer, then herded them out of the cabin. Some still grumbled about their wet hair, *but they were on time.*

By Thursday the entire camp bristled with excitement. That evening marked the debut of the teen banquet. This year's expo theme would be enhanced by the artistic talents of Daryn Brock, who was busily painting the lodge's windows with scenes from various countries. Other staff members, hiding from the campers' view, stretched their mouths out of shape by blowing up a hundred balloons that would fill a giant basket suspended from the lodge's ceiling. The kitchen crew labored hard over their stoves. Everyone wanted to make the banquet an evening to remember.

All of Becka's girls had dates for the event, except one—Noreen. She was tiny, with fine features.

"Don't worry!" Becka consoled her. "You can be my date tonight."

Becka joined the "primpers," because she, too, wanted to look her best. She selected the lavender-and-white dress she had worn on class night for her academy graduation. Then she recurled her hair at the shower house.

Finally, she and Noreen followed the crowd to the lodge, where the cafeteria had been transformed into an enchanting banquet hall. Different-colored tablecloths glowed under candlelight as the campers found their places.

Becka immediately caught Geoff's attention. "Hello!" she said. "Meet my date, Noreen!"

Geoff's blue eyes gleamed at the small, porcelainlike girl at Becka's side. "Hi, Noreen!" he said. "Can I be your date too?" he asked.

"Yes," she responded shyly, blushing.

Geoff plopped down between the two girls and proceeded to make their evening an interesting one. He seemed to take great care in paying more attention to Noreen than to Becka, which the girl's counselor welcomed. At the same time, she liked sitting so close to him in such a romantic setting.

A film about the Olympics began about 9:30. Before long, however, several of Becka's girls grew tired of the festivities and began to mill around. Trisha was first to approach the counselor. "May I go back to the cabin and change my dress?" she asked.

"Why? You look very pretty in that one," Becka said.

"But someone else has on a dress just like this one," the girl complained.

"Sorry!" Becka held her ground. "Maxine said no one can return to the cabins until after the film."

Next Cheryl and Noreen stood before her, pleading to return to the cabin.

"I'm really sorry," Becka repeated, "but Maxine has ordered us all to stay here until . . ."

"But we're tired and want to go to sleep," Cheryl argued.

Becka wanted to cry out, "I'm tired and want to go to sleep too!" Instead, she sympathized with the girls, but sent them back to their seats. Her eyes squinted in the darkened room. She was finding it more and more difficult to keep track of all twelve of her campers.

Next Candis emerged from the crowd with her woe. "I have a miserable cold, my head aches, I'm coughing, sneezing, and I want to go to bed."

"Can you wait for just half an hour?" Becka pleaded.

"I guess so," Candis said with a sigh.

At long last the film ended, and Becka took her place by the door.

"Cabin 13!" she called in her loudest, most authoritative voice. When only a few of her campers straggled wearily to her side, she called again, "Cabin 13!" After two more calls, she counted eleven girls.

Becka cringed when she realized—Candis was missing!

Chapter 8

Blind Camp

Back at the cabin they found the missing camper curled up in her bunk, sound asleep.

A sudden flush of anger warmed Becka. "Candis disobeyed me," she thought. "I should wake her up." But then a wave of sympathy checked her as she gazed at the sleeping girl.

"She's feeling sick," she mused, remembering how miserable she herself had felt the week before.

Just then Becka noticed Cheryl climbing into her sleeping bag, still clothed in her banquet dress. "Cheryl! You need to get into your pajamas."

The camper responded with a boisterous giggle.

"Cheryl!" Becka's voice sounded firmer. "Come on, out of that bag and into your pajamas!"

"*Har! Har! Har!*" the camper laughed again and slumped to the floor like a lifeless rag doll.

Suddenly Becka felt very young, very small, and very weary. "Let no man despise thy youth; but be thou an example of the believers, in word . . . in charity, in faith . . ."

After much coaxing, Becka convinced Cheryl to change into her nightclothes, then gathered everyone—except Candis—into a circle on the floor. All through the story and prayer Cheryl tried to keep a lid on her giggles, but they poked through now and then anyway, sending suppressed laughter throughout the giddy group. The outbreak didn't end with lights-out, either. More giggles erupted until 1:30 in the morning.

"And I have to get up in exactly three hours," Becka thought in disgust.

At daybreak the counselor didn't feel the least bit refreshed. She dragged herself through the rest of the week's activities until Sunday morning, when she helped her campers pack for their return home.

Energy had seeped back into her bones, though, by the time her Teen 2 girls arrived. At once she realized that her cabin was filling with a group of comedians. Janet did funny impressions of a popular TV star. Dark-haired Karissa squealed, "Whoo! Whoo!" whenever the urge hit her.

Karissa's friend, Mindy, however, stood out amidst the clowns, not because of any impressions she did or jokes she told, but because Mindy was quiet, introspective—"and beautiful!" Becka mused.

Sally was the first in their cabin to get hurt. She twisted her foot in gymnastics and had to rely on crutches the rest of the week. And every afternoon at least three of Becka's girls had to visit the nurse's office for one ailment or another.

"I've got a cabinful of klutzes!" the counselor complained to Geoff one morning during their worship hour. He suggested they have special prayer for her girls.

"We'd better pray harder," Becka announced the next morning. "Another of my girls is on crutches!"

"Oh, no!" he moaned. "You *did* end up with all the accident-prone ones this time."

Thursday evening all of her girls had dressed in their finest apparel and had set out for line call, awaiting the walk with their dates to the teen banquet, except one—Mindy.

Taller than Becka, Mindy slumped on her bed, looking crestfallen. Her long blond hair, feathered back from her face, revealed perfectly proportioned features and a flawless complexion.

"I look ugly," she blurted. "I can't go out there."

Becka's jaw dropped in astonishment. "Ugly?" she exclaimed. "Mindy, you're one of the prettiest girls in Teen 2 camp! I'm shocked that you would feel that way."

Mindy started to cry. "Well, I feel like I look ugly, and I just can't go out there."

In a desperate voice, Becka begged, "Mindy, they'll be lowering the flag in a minute, and I'm not there. Please, can't you take my word for it? You really *do* look pretty."

The other girl clutched her pillow. She shook her head emphatically. "No! I just can't go out there looking like this."

Becka felt more bewildered, realizing that nothing she could tell the teenager in those few moments would erase the low self-image stamped in her mind.

The counselor eyed the girl's Quaker-knit sweater and full green skirt. Here was a beautiful young woman dressed in the latest fashion, whose low self-esteem prevented her from enjoying a wonderful evening. When Becka heard the bugle blowing, closing the flag-lowering ceremonies, anxiety twisted her stomach into knots. "My girls are without a leader."

"I'll just have to get the girls' director—" she began.

"No!" Mindy pleaded tearfully. "I'll go, but—but—please, stay close to me."

"I will," Becka promised.

As she trudged alongside Mindy toward the banquet hall, the counselor felt a tinge of frustration. "Sometimes I wish I could follow these girls home," she thought, "and help them gain some confidence in themselves."

Becka instantly recognized the irony in her thinking, and the next morning she shared her thoughts with

Beth at their usual place in the shower house. "I, of all people, should understand how poor Mindy feels. I didn't have much confidence myself at the beginning of teen camp."

Beth countered with her cheer-filled voice, "Who does? It's scary for any counselor as young as us to be in charge of kids so close to our own ages."

"Well, just the same, I'm ashamed to think how much I dreaded teen camp," Becka confessed. "And here I am hating to say goodbye to them today. I've really enjoyed these girls."

Beth snickered. "Enjoy your last precious moments with them, because our work really begins in a few hours."

"What do you mean?" Becka asked.

"Blind camp, my dear!"

"But, Beth," Becka retorted, "I've looked forward to blind camp for years. I would think that helping blind children enjoy outdoor life would be a most rewarding and—and—exhilarating experience."

"Rewarding? Yes," Beth replied. "Exhilarating? No!" Her voice broke into a halfhearted laugh. "I'd say *exhausting* would better describe the experience." Then she turned and pointed her curling iron at Becka's nose. "You'll see," she warned. "You'll see."

That day, as soon as the last teenager boarded the bus for home, the camp hummed with activity. Staff workers strung rope from each of the cabins to the shower houses. When they finished, the camp looked like a giant weaver had dropped his loom amidst the trees. This maze of ropes would guide the arriving blind campers safely to and from the bathrooms that week.

Coincidentally, Beth and Becka were paired together as counselors for a cabin of five sightless girls. Becka helped Doris, Claudia, and Lucy roll out their sleeping bags and put away their belongings while Beth did the same with Loretta and Hallie.

Immediately, everyone realized that Hallie was not only blind, but she suffered from several other conditions. Becka's heart sank when she recognized the familiar behavior of an autistic cousin named Ozzie, who had lived with her family for three years. She noticed the constant rocking of her head, the grunting sounds, the girl's extreme stubbornness, and her refusal to venture into Becka's world. Hallie was "tripping out"—a form of self-hypnosis that kept her securely inside her own head, where she didn't have to face these strange, new surroundings.

"Mr. Teague, the man in charge of all these kids, told me that Hallie is severely retarded and autistic as well as blind," Beth whispered.

"I was afraid of that," Becka replied. "Just like my cousin, Ozzie."

Beth gave her a hopeful glance. "Then you know how to take care of her?"

"It's not that simple," Becka whispered back. Then she held her breath and asked, "Do you know if she's potty-trained?"

"Mr. Teague said she was."

Becka sighed with relief, then turned her attention toward the loud moans erupting from Hallie's bunk as the girl repeatedly rocked her body back and forth.

Noting the concern in the faces of the other campers, she called out cheerfully, "Come on, girls! Beth will sit on the floor with you in a circle and tell you all about the camp rules and the great fun you're going to have this week."

Becka gently pulled Hallie's hand and tried to coax her off the bed, but the girl wouldn't budge. The counselor tugged harder, but Hallie continued to rock back and forth, moaning.

Becka then used both hands and put all of her weight

into the task of rooting Hallie out of the bed. The girl moved, but not without loud moans of protest.

Meanwhile, Beth had begun her speech about camp life. Her voice grew louder and louder, competing with Hallie's noise. Finally, she stopped talking. Her eyes silently pleaded with her partner, "Can't you do something?"

Becka remembered how she had handled Ozzie, who was much smaller than this big teenage girl. "Come on, Hallie!" she exclaimed. "Sit on my lap!"

Hallie plopped her body ungraciously onto Becka's lap.

"Ugh!" Becka felt her breath escape as the oversized girl pressed her into the floor. Squirming uncomfortably under the heavy weight, Becka almost giggled at the prospect of Beth having to pry her off the floor with a pancake turner.

As the evening progressed, Becka took complete charge of Hallie while Beth guided the other four girls—and a seeing-eye dog—to line call, then to supper.

Becka managed to keep ahold of the autistic youngster with one hand and balance a tray of food with the other. Setting Hallie before her dinner, she placed a fork in the girl's hand. "Time to eat!" she singsonged.

Bang! The fork flew across the table and hit a bench.

Bang! Bang! Bang! The girl drummed the spoon on her tray.

"Oh, no!" Becka gasped. "Now she's tripping out on—"

The spoon flew across the table. Then Becka looked on in exasperation while Hallie plunged into her mashed potatoes with all ten fingers and began shoveling the mush into her mouth, smacking her lips loudly while she licked her fingers.

"Just let her alone!" Beth ordered. "You go ahead and eat while you have a chance!"

Becka wrinkled up her nose. "I think I just lost my appetite."

All during campfire time Becka struggled with Hallie on her lap, trying to keep her quiet during the skits. "These campers can't *see* the actors, so they have to be able to hear what they're saying," Becka whispered to the girl. But Hallie ignored her—or simply didn't understand.

Bedtime grew worse. Hallie caused such a commotion that no one could sleep—not even the dog. When the girl finally drifted off, Becka found herself jerking awake every few minutes. She harbored a deep fear that Hallie might awaken, wander outside, and get lost in the woods.

Memories of her cousin kept her company that long, sleepless night. She recalled the weeks it took to teach him to eat with a spoon and the tedious hours of trying to get him to say just one word.

When the little autistic boy would finally make some progress, the entire family would clap and cheer for him. But there was no family to cheer at Camp Wautum Woods—no mother to take over when Becka grew weary of washing and dressing this oversized doll named Hallie.

"Her poor parents!" Becka thought. "How continuously tired they must be with a daughter like this!" The counselor took some comfort in knowing that at least she was giving Hallie's parents some much-needed rest that week.

After two nights of little sleep, Becka came close to tears when she shared the problem with Geoff at their special place by the lake.

"Maybe you should go to Pastor Joe about the problems you're having with Hallie," he suggested.

"I can't, Geoff!" Becka sighed. "With all the trouble my other campers have had—Ruzena's leaving, the tardy ones, then the klutzes—Pastor Joe probably already thinks I'm a disaster as a counselor. This thing with Hallie would only convince him he's right." She caught her breath, then blurted, "He'll never hire me back next year."

"Becka," Geoff nearly reached for her hand, but caught himself, "you can't continue to go without sleep like this. And what about your other campers? Have you considered how much she must be spoiling their fun?"

Becka looked glumly down at the waves sloshing against the shore. "Couldn't we just pray about it for now?" she asked in a timid voice. Inside, however, she wondered how long she could cope with Hallie.

A few minutes later the hill looked as impossible to climb as an unscalable cliff when Becka dragged her tired body to her cabin to awaken Hallie, guide her to the shower house, wash her, dress her, and brush the girl's teeth and hair. The day crawled by in a meaningless blur. But by afternoon she seemed to catch a second wind and a sudden surge of "supercounseloritis" when she and Beth led their girls down to the lakeside.

"OK, Hallie!" Becka said enthusiastically. "You might not understand much about camp life, but I think you could enjoy a canoe ride if you tried."

Carefully, the counselor strapped the girl into a life preserver and put her near the floor of the canoe, on a soft bed of life jackets. Next Becka began to paddle the canoe away from the dock and toward the swim dock several hundred yards away.

"Isn't this fun, Hallie?" she chirped.

The handicapped girl stared blankly at the water surrounding her. Then a strange gleam entered her eye and, without warning, she began to rock the canoe wildly, making Becka's surge of "supercounseloritis" evaporate in an instant.

"Stop!" Becka screamed.

But Hallie was deeply engrossed in this new way of "tripping out." Back and forth she rocked the canoe until it tipped dangerously.

Becka paddled faster toward the swim dock. "Hallieeee! I don't want to fish you out of this la-a-ake!"

Hallie continued to rock, blissfully unaware of the danger she was causing.

Becka reached the dock just in time to steady the canoe with her hand, which sent Hallie into a howl of protest. Quickly, while the blind girl seemed preoccupied with her own voice, Becka picked up the paddle and moved swift strokes back toward the canoe dock.

When she and Hallie safely reached the shore, Becka grinned sheepishly at Beth, who stood speechless, waiting. "Well, so much for Hallie's enjoying camp life!" Becka said.

"You tried," Beth replied, then helped one of the other girls into the canoe.

That evening at campfire time, Becka was so exhausted she barely had the strength to keep Hallie on her lap. When the handicapped youngster seemed louder than usual, the counselor marched her to the rear seats. But then the girl really howled, digging her sharp fingernails into Becka's arms, scratching bloody trails from her elbows to her wrists.

Tears of pain rushed to Becka's eyes. "That's it, Hallie! You're going to bed." She pulled the noisy teenager up the hill to the shower house and put her in a toilet stall.

"Go to the bathroom, Hallie!" she ordered, then turned to the sink and washed her wounds with soap and water.

Her arms were stinging when she heard the toilet flush.

"Good girl, Hallie," Becka said as she opened the door to the stall. "Oh, no!"

Both of Hallie's shoes were floating in the toilet!

Chapter 9

Hallie

Angry tears splashed down Becka's cheeks. What was that Bible verse? "Be thou an example . . ." "Please, Lord, don't let anyone see me like this!" Becka had never felt so angry. "Help me, Lord!" she prayed under her breath.

With two fingers she gingerly fished the soggy shoes out of the toilet, then washed them as best she could in a sink. Barefooted and grunting like a contented piglet, Hallie traipsed back to the cabin alongside her unusually quiet counselor. Becka dressed the girl in her pajamas, all the while lecturing her about the evils of throwing her shoes in the toilet and about "yucky germs."

Hallie responded by clapping her hands together like a performing seal, obviously not understanding a word.

When Beth arrived with the rest of the girls, Becka told her, "While they get ready for bed, I'm going to find Pastor Joe."

In answer to her friend's questioning look, Becka whispered, "I've got to tell him what's happening. I can't go through another night without sleep." Her mouth twisted into a sardonic smile. "After all, what would it look like on my job résumé—'as a counselor at Camp Wautum Woods, I totally freaked out'?"

Once Becka made her way through the maze of guide ropes, she sprinted over the darkened trails like a frightened deer, straight to the director's cabin. When he opened his door, she looked into his surprised face and blurted, "I need some encouragement and wisdom." Then the whole wretched story tumbled out about the last three grueling days with Hallie.

Pastor Joe invited Becka in and calmly informed her, "If you want to know the truth, I asked Mr. Teague not to bring Hallie back to camp this year. We had similar problems with her last summer."

He paused, looking lost in thought. "Don't get me wrong! I'm all for the mentally handicapped enjoying camp also. But, honestly, I think that girl would be just as contented elsewhere and not really know the difference."

"I feel so sorry for her parents," Becka put in. "I know they desperately need the rest."

"Yes, but at whose expense?" Pastor Joe replied. "Obviously, she's upsetting the other girls. It's not fair to them," he said, leaning back against a chair.

All her pent-up anxiety about Pastor Joe's impression of her started to melt away as he continued, "Mr. Teague must have forgotten my request about Hallie. I'll go fetch him, and we'll have a little powwow—now."

Gulp! Becka hadn't expected such a drastic reaction. This could prove uncomfortable for her.

Minutes later she squirmed uneasily as Pastor Joe told the other director, "I hire the best, and I don't want my counselors burned out emotionally and physically because of a child who would probably be just as happy in a professional respite program. It's not fair to the other campers, either." On and on he talked, while feelings of elation, sorrow, relief, and embarrassment swam in and out of Becka's weary mind.

Pastor Joe concluded his speech with orders for Becka:

"If you have any more problems with Hallie, anything at all, you just go get Mr. Teague here, and he'll help you."

"I'd be glad to," the other man said.

Becka felt sorry for him. After all, his intentions had been noble ones—to give Hallie a camping experience while at the same time providing her parents with some relief. Right now, though, all she wanted was to crawl into her bunk and get some sleep, undisturbed the entire night through. But that was not to be.

When she returned to the cabin, Becka found all the girls in an uproar because Hallie was screaming and banging her head against the wall. Immediately, she backtracked, this time heading to Headquarters Building, where she soon found Mr. Teague's room. As soon as he opened the door, she put on her panicked-counselor look and exclaimed, "Hallie's screaming and banging her head against the wall. She's keeping all the girls awake, and Beth and I don't know what's wrong with her."

Grabbing his coat, Mr. Teague said, "I'll get the doctor, and we'll meet you back at your cabin."

Ten minutes later the two men rapped on the cabin door, then entered. The doctor had a kind, soothing voice. "The girl's behavior means she's got a headache. I have some medication for her." He handed her some pills.

Hallie gobbled them down, then slowly stopped her rocking and noisemaking. As suddenly as the episode had begun, it stopped. The girl laid her head on her pillow and fell asleep.

But Becka, as tired as she was, still couldn't rest comfortably. It seemed that one ear listened all night for the slightest sound, jolting her awake again and again. The next day Kathy Stevens came to her rescue. "Pastor Joe sent me to care for Hallie until Mandy can take over."

"Mandy? From the horse corral?" Becka looked puzzled.

"She's strong, Becka, and she's really sweet." Kathy smiled sympathetically. "Everyone knows what you've been going through. And I, for one, think you're made of pretty tough stuff to have endured so long."

Becka smiled back. Now she could relax and enjoy her other campers. But she didn't dare relax too much, or she would surely fall asleep on her feet.

Becka wondered about the golden labrador that belonged to Claudia. The seeing-eye dog kept bumbling around camp, leading his blind owner into poles and trees.

"Maybe he's better at home in familiar surroundings," Becka hoped.

Loretta, her camper with long, curly blond hair, won Becka's affection immediately. Wearing glasses, Loretta could see out of one eye. The girl had just graduated from high school, so she was a year older than Becka. But that didn't change her sweet and helpful demeanor.

Lucy and Doris also proved to be fun, and Becka began to enjoy "counseling" again, while Mandy and Kathy took turns struggling with Hallie.

Claudia, who was totally blind and much older than all of her cabinmates, must have decided that things had settled down too much for her liking, and that she needed to refuel the fires of excitement. Wednesday evening, when Becka told the girls to hurry into their bedclothes because the camp pastor was coming for their worship time, Claudia deliberately dawdled.

Becka gently reminded her, "The pastor will be here in ten minutes, and you'll need to be in your pajamas and sleeping bag before he walks through that door."

The blind girl fingered the nightclothes in her lap, but ignored Becka and continued talking.

Five minutes passed, and Claudia was still sitting and chattering atop her bunk. Becka tried again. "Claudia, you'd better hurry—"

"I can't hurry!" the older girl snapped, pounding her fist on the mattress. "Hurrying makes me nervous."

"Well, then, don't hurry," Becka told her, "but get changed as fast as you can!"

A few snickers rose from the other beds while Claudia began to grumble, "I hate hurrying. I hate this place. Counselors much younger than I am think they can boss me around."

"I'm sorry you feel that way," Becka said, but she wanted to say, "When you act like a grade schooler, then you get treated like a grade schooler."

On and on Claudia complained, but she did it while changing her clothes, so Becka let her ramble.

At long last the older girl slipped into her sleeping bag and zipped it up.

"Yea! She's in bed," Becka cheered while everyone clapped.

But Claudia mumbled, "Yeah, but my nerves are shot."

At that, Becka stuffed part of her pillow into her mouth to keep her giggles from escaping.

When she awoke Thursday morning, Becka had slept so hard she told herself, "This must be what it feels like to come out of a coma." She fairly flew down to the edge of the lake, where Geoff waited for their worship time. He was ecstatic about Mandy's mission as "angel of mercy" for the distraught counselor. "I was seriously concerned about your sanity, Becka." When she laughed, he chided her, "I'm not kidding. You know what our church preaches about health. Our bodies are truly the temples of the Holy Spirit, and we need to keep them in tiptop shape."

She smiled faintly, remembering a similar speech once made by her academy friend, Marty Webster.

Becka listened until Geoff finished sermonizing, then said, "Our day off starts this evening. Where shall we spend our last moments together before . . ."

Geoff's mood changed abruptly. "Uh, I hate to tell you this, but they didn't make my day off the same time as yours this week."

"They didn't?" She felt heartsick. I guess that means we won't have any time together away from camp then, huh?"

Geoff nodded. "And I have to leave Sunday morning. My folks are coming then."

At those words they both fell silent. A whole year faced them—a year of being separated by 2,000 miles. Becka felt like throwing her arms around his neck and crying softly on his shoulder, but that would destroy their well-polished act as just two friends at Camp Wautum Woods, simply sharing their morning worships together.

Geoff was first to break the silence. "Do you realize our evaluations come up in just a few days?"

"Yes," she said. "Then we'll find out whether or not they want us back next year." In that moment, however, being rehired the following summer didn't seem as important. All she could think of was their goodbye only three days off.

Chapter 10

Goodbye, Geoff

Wrapped in a bulky blanket, Becka looked like a squaw huddled by the lake. Three of their friends splashed in the darkening waters, seemingly oblivious to the setting sun and the cooling air that stirred the forest around them.

"Whew!" Jake Shepherd emerged from the lake and grabbed a beach towel. "That'll keep me awake awhile!" Then he noticed Becka's somber mood. "Hey! Cheer up! This is your night off."

"I know," Becka said. "It's just that summer's coming to an end soon. I hate saying goodbye to all my Camp-Wautum-Woods friends. And Texas is *so* far away."

Jake wrapped the towel around his shoulders and plopped down beside her. "It gets worse in college."

"It does?"

"Yep! Good buddies marry or go off to a mission field. It seems like the older you get, the more often you have to say goodbye." Without warning, he yelled to Connie and Jill, "You two had better come out of there before the Loch Ness monster gets you!"

The two girls squealed, but continued swimming.

"They sure mind well." He chuckled, then turned his attention back to Becka. "It's all part of growing up—

saying goodbye, I mean."

Becka sighed. "I guess so, but I don't have to *like* it." She and Jake continued their talk until the thick forest grew so dark they could hardly see.

"OK, that's it," Jake shouted into the night. "You girls come out of the lake right now before you die of hypothermia!"

Connie and Jill came splashing and giggling out of the water, deliberately dribbling onto "bossy" Jake. Then they all piled into Connie's car and drove back to camp.

Becka still felt glum. She wished she could talk with Geoff, but he was on duty, busy with his cabinful of sightless boys. She climbed the steps to the staff lounge and sank down on the carpet, deep in thought. "Maybe I shouldn't go so far away to college. Maybe I should stay closer to home . . . and closer to Geoff. . . . "

A loud clamoring up the stairs brought Dan Burnett and Sean Snow to her side.

"What are you doing up here all alone?" Dan asked.

"Just thinking."

Dan took out a note pad and began to write, mumbling, "Becka Bailey was found thinking in the staff lounge."

The girl laughed. "What's that for?"

"Our report. We're watchmen tonight." Dan caressed a nightstick at his side. "See, I even have a beanie-bopper in case we run into a burglar."

Becka laughed again. "A burglar? Clear up here in the middle of nowhere? What an imagination!"

Dan looked insulted, but Sean retrieved his ego with, "Oh, he might need to use it on a vicious bear."

"Yeah," Dan echoed him, "a *mean*, vicious bear."

Becka played along, looking quite sober. "The worst kind!"

The boys turned to leave, then stopped abruptly. "Becka," Sean asked, "since you're not doing anything but thinking on your night off, why don't you join Dan and me on our rounds? You could be watchwoman."

Surprising herself, Becka exclaimed, "Sure! Why not? I'll carry the flashlight."

"Great!" Sean studied his checklist. "Next is the parking lot."

Becka followed the two guys, illuminating their path with the wide beam of light. Suddenly, they heard sawdust crunching ahead.

"Halt!" Dan ordered dramatically. "Who goes there?"

A deep voice spoke from the dark, "Brad Mason. I'm on my way into town to phone my folks."

"OK! Goodbye!" Sean called back.

Becka shined the flashlight on Dan's note pad while he wrote about the incident.

Next the jolly threesome made their way to the horse stables.

Snort! A horse beckoned to them—a horse that had escaped from his stall and was wandering around loose in the corral. So the three of them pushed, pulled, coaxed, and prodded the horse, but to no avail.

Dan huffed, "This guy's got to be part mule."

"*Part*?" Sean asked in exasperation. "I think he's *all* mule—in disguise."

"Yeah," the other fellow agreed. "He's probably had plastic surgery on his ears."

Dan took out the familiar note pad while Becka watched her fellow *Hiawatha* actor write in Indian jargon:

> We come up
> See horse out
> Try to put horse in stall
> Horse no go
> We decide horse to stay out of stall
> We leave.

Just as they turned from the stables, they heard a rustling sound in the trees nearby. Instinctively, Becka shined the light in that direction, revealing a deer. The doe's ears and nose twitched at them, her pensive, dark eyes looking curious, then bored as if thinking, "It's just those silly camp staffers out playing nightwatchpeople again."

Becka held her breath. She stood in awe of the wild creature standing only four feet from her. All the while Dan and Sean crept stealthily closer.

Just as they were ready to pounce on the deer, the animal leapt into the air and disappeared in a flash.

"Aw!" Sean groaned. "I wanted to catch her and take her home with me."

At long last they completed their rounds of the entire camp, and Becka said goodnight at the staff cabin.

The next morning she splashed cold water on her face, crammed her contact lenses into her eyes, then sped down to the lake, where Geoff was waiting.

"Some of us are being evaluated today," he told her.

Becka's heart fluttered nervously. "So this is it. We'll find out if the directors suspect anything between us and if they plan to rehire us next summer."

After their Bible study and prayer, she returned to her cabin and slept until noon.

Sooner than she wished, Becka stood before the evaluation board.

Pastor Joe was first to speak. "Becka, initially I wasn't too sure about your ability, because you're much younger than the other counselors. Also, your attitude seemed a little negative at first." He continued, spelling out the adversities she had faced and the problems she had solved. "I've seen real growth in you this summer. You've turned into an excellent counselor."

Maxine was next with her evaluation sheet. She had given Becka high marks on everything. "I've appreciated your willingness to fill in for a sick counselor or anywhere else I've asked," the girls' director commented. "I know I can depend on you at a moment's notice."

"Thank you," Becka replied. Her voice sounded calm, but inside, her stomach churned. "Do they know how Geoff and I feel about each other?" she wondered.

When the boys' director finished speaking, Pastor Joe said bluntly, "Now, about Geoffrey Blake . . ."

He knew all the time! Here it comes. Becka stiffened, bracing herself against the inevitable words: "Because you disobeyed the rule about staff romances, we cannot hire you back next year."

Instead, the camp director surprised her with, "You handled your relationship very wisely. The campers never suspected your true feelings, and that's what matters. Both you and Geoff acted quite professional and in a Christian manner at all times."

Becka thought, "It's a good thing he didn't witness my performance when Hallie tried to flush her shoes down the toilet!"

"Under those circumstances," Pastor Joe concluded, "I would feel very comfortable about rehiring you for next summer."

Becka couldn't contain her glee another minute.

"Thank you!" Her reply sounded too loud as she spun around and headed back to her cabin. To her dismay, she quickly drifted off to sleep and nearly missed relieving her sub at line call.

"I've never slept so much in one day!" she told Beth at suppertime.

"You're just making up for all those sleepless nights with Hallie," her friend said.

On Sabbath Becka received another surprise—her father and brother had come to say goodbye. "Mom will be here tomorrow night," Kurt said. "She's all packed and ready for the big trip to Texas."

Sunday morning Becka dashed to the lakeshore, wanting to savor every last moment with Geoff. Next to Beth, he had become Becka's closest friend.

Sadly, they discussed their Bible lesson, then bowed while each prayed a prayer of praise and guidance for their futures.

With the "amen," Geoff gently took Becka's face in his hands and kissed her.

"Geoff!" she chided him. "They'll take back their promise to rehire us and—and what about the campers?"

Geoff grinned. "They're blind, remember?"

Becka reddened. Sometimes her boyfriend's sense of humor seemed warped. She lowered her head and tried to analyze her feelings. Why was she suddenly feeling angry? She decided she wasn't really angry at Geoff. She was angry at the 2,000 lonely miles that would separate them.

The next few hours were crammed with packing for her girls, helping them with the last-minute tasks before they boarded the bus. She hugged each camper with extra fervor—even Hallie, who seemed lost again in her own protected world. Any kind of change was hard on kids like Hallie, Becka thought.

As soon as the bus pulled away, Becka and Beth raced back to their cabin to clean it thoroughly.

With a heavy heart, Becka stirred up a cloud of dust as she swept the floor. "Mama always said work's a sure cure for a heartache—" She was interrupted by a knock at the door.

"Geoff!"

He talked rapidly, nonstop, "Becka, my folks are here, and I asked them about it, and they said I could go ahead and do what I wanted. It's OK with them."

"W-what are you talking about?" she stammered.

"Texas!" Geoff exclaimed, his eyes dancing with amusement. "I'm going to your college in Texas—that is, *if* you can find me a job first."

Becka gasped. "I'll find you a job as soon as I get down there," she promised.

"I'll be eagerly awaiting your call," he said, slipping her his address and phone number. With his salutation, " 'Bye, girls!" he was gone.

Becka squealed with delight and hugged Beth. Then her broom really stirred up the dust.

That evening when her mother arrived, they stuffed every nook and cranny of the car with Becka's gear, until there was barely enough room for the two of them. Several of Becka's friends, including Beth, were there to see her off. Now she was the one pulling away from Camp Wautum Woods, with "Goodbye! Goodbye!" echoing through the tall firs.

Moonlight streamed along the bumpy road ahead of them, like a silver carpet welcoming her to a new adventure. College ahead, camp behind, where she had learned so much about responsibility and about people—little people as well as adults. Camp, where she had learned to love even the unlovable. Where her prayers grew feet and helping hands. Where she had fallen in love with Geoffrey Blake.

Becka sighed. It seemed she had aged several years that summer. With new confidence she faced the future.